W9-BBC-364

Searchlight
BOOKS™

How Does
Government
Work?

The President, Vice President, and Cabinet

A Look at the Executive Branch

Elaine Landau

Lerner Publications Company
Minneapolis

Lerner Publications Company
A division of Lerner Publishing Group, Inc.
241 First Avenue North
Minneapolis, MN 55401 U.S.A.

Website address: www.lernerbooks.com

Library of Congress Cataloging-in-Publication Data

Landau, Elaine.
    The President, Vice President, and Cabinet : A look at the executive branch / by
Elaine Landau.
        p.   cm. — (Searchlight books™—How does government work?)
    Includes index.
    ISBN 978–0–7613–6517–4 (lib. bdg. : alk. paper)
    1. Presidents—United States—Juvenile literature. 2. Executive departments—
United States—Juvenile literature. I. Title.
JK517.L36 2012
352.230973—dc22   2010041799

Manufactured in the United States of America
1 – DP – 12/31/11

Contents

Chapter 1

BECOMING PRESIDENT

The president does important work. He or she helps make the country's laws. The president also directs foreign policy. This means he or she decides how the country will relate to other nations. Leading the military is part of the president's job too.

A family listens to President John F. Kennedy speak on television in the 1960s. What are some of the president's jobs?

Who Can Be President?

To be president, you must be a U.S. citizen. You must have been born in the United States. You must have lived in the United States for at least fourteen years. And you must be at least thirty-five years old.

Barack Obama became president when he was forty-seven years old.

THESE CITIZENS ARE VOTING FOR PRESIDENT.

Presidents are elected. This means citizens choose them by voting. Presidents are elected for four-year terms. A president can serve up to two terms.

The Oath

Presidents must promise to take their duties seriously.
This promise is called the oath of office. Serving the
country is an honor. But being president is also a job.
The president gets paid for his or her work.

**Ronald Reagan (LEFT)
takes the oath of
office in 1981 as his
wife, Nancy, looks on.**

Congress decides how much the president gets paid. Congress is made up of the Senate and the House of Representatives. In 2001, Congress decided the president should make $400,000 a year.

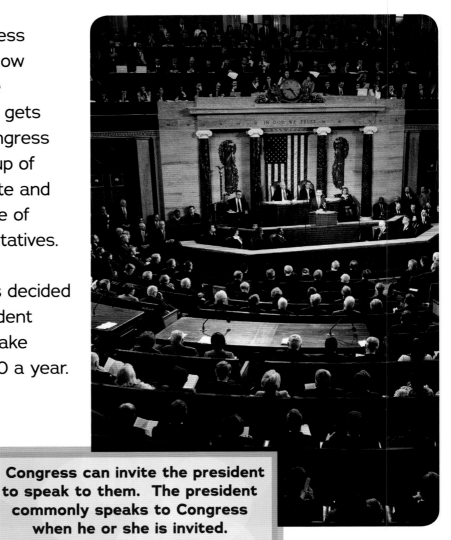

Congress can invite the president to speak to them. The president commonly speaks to Congress when he or she is invited.

Tough Job

Presidents can be asked to make decisions day or night. They often work seven days a week. Their job has no limits.

President Gerald R. Ford works at his desk in the White House in 1975.

People can't fire the president if they don't think he or she is doing a good job. But Congress can remove a president from office if Congress thinks he or she has done something very wrong.

President Richard Nixon was almost removed from office in 1974. He was caught covering up for his employees, who stole information to help him get reelected. Nixon left the presidency before Congress could remove him from office.

To remove a president from office, the House of Representatives must impeach the president. This means they have to accuse him or her of wrongdoing. Then the Senate must decide if he or she is guilty. To remove a president from office, two-thirds of the Senate must say the president is guilty.

Chapter 2

GOVERNMENT BRANCHES

The president is one of the world's most powerful people. Leading the United States is a big job.

The president has a lot of power. But our nation's founders didn't give the president total power. Do you know why?

Our nation's founders wanted a strong president. But they didn't want the president to be all-powerful. They wanted a leader who would help all Americans reach their goals.

President George Washington (RIGHT) talks to Alexander Hamilton (CENTER) and Thomas Jefferson (LEFT) in 1795. These men are some of our nation's founders.

Three Parts

Our founders designed the government to have three parts. The parts are called branches. They are the executive branch, the legislative branch, and the judicial branch.

The U.S. Constitution defines the roles of each branch of government.

MEMBERS OF CONGRESS APPLAUD PRESIDENT OBAMA AS HE MAKES A SPEECH IN 2011.

The president leads the executive branch. Congress makes up the legislative branch. The Supreme Court (the nation's highest court) and other federal courts make up the judicial branch.

Power is divided among the branches. This way of ruling keeps any one branch from becoming too powerful.

The branches keep presidents, such as Theodore Roosevelt, from taking too much control.

Executive Branch

The president is called the chief executive. That's because he or she heads the executive branch. That's a huge responsibility. Our founders knew the president couldn't do it alone.

President Ronald Reagan works on a report in 1986. The president has a lot of work, so he has help.

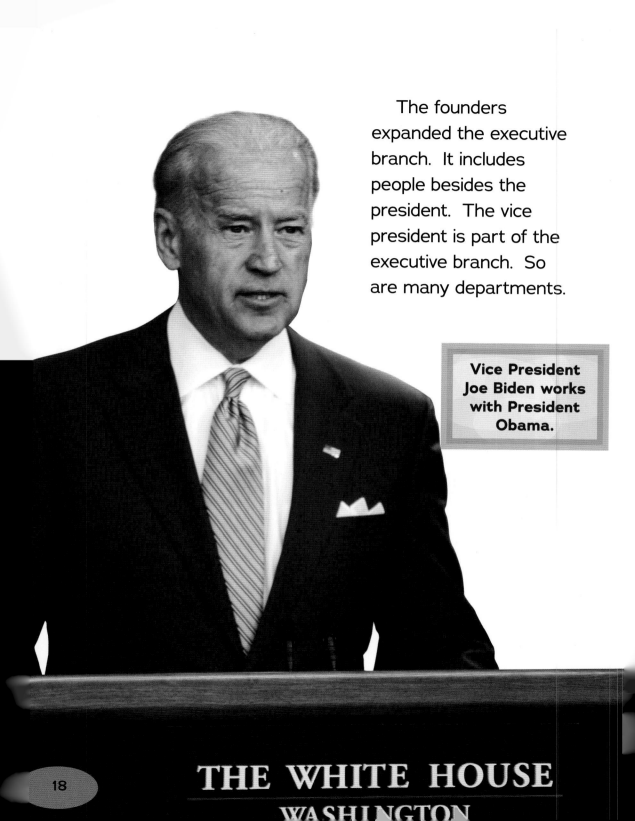

The founders expanded the executive branch. It includes people besides the president. The vice president is part of the executive branch. So are many departments.

Vice President Joe Biden works with President Obama.

THE WHITE HOUSE
WASHINGTON

The departments help the president run the government. The department heads help with issues in specific areas. The department heads are called the president's cabinet.

PRESIDENT DWIGHT EISENHOWER'S CABINET MEETS IN 1954.

Chapter 3

BILLS

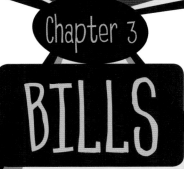

Presidents can't make laws by themselves. Presidents can only suggest bills. A bill is an idea for a new law.

A worker picks up a bill about health care. What is a bill?

Bills go to Congress to be passed into law. All presidents want their bills to become laws. Presidents try to convince Congress to pass their bills.

President Herbert Hoover speaks to Congress in 1932.

Approving Bills

Presidents do more than try to talk Congress into passing bills. The president also signs bills that Congress passes. When a president signs a bill, it becomes a law.

In 1964, President Lyndon Johnson signs a bill giving rights to Americans of all races. Before this law, African Americans and other minorities weren't able to exercise the same rights as white Americans.

A president can also decide to veto a bill. *Veto* means "to reject." Congress can override, or vote to cancel, a president's veto. But that doesn't happen often.

President George H. W. Bush (SEATED) looks over a bill next to Vice President Dan Quayle in 1991.

Chapter 4

CHIEF EXECUTIVE

In addition to signing bills, the president has emergency powers. These powers give the president the ability to prevent or deal with national emergencies. The president also has the power to uphold laws. And he or she makes sure treaties are carried out. Treaties are agreements with other nations.

President Bill Clinton comforts a victim of a 1993 flood in Iowa. Presidents use emergency powers in such situations. What are emergency powers?

Tools

The president has tools to do all this. One tool is issuing an executive order. Executive orders are as powerful as laws. They don't have to be approved by Congress. The president can also call out the army to enforce a law.

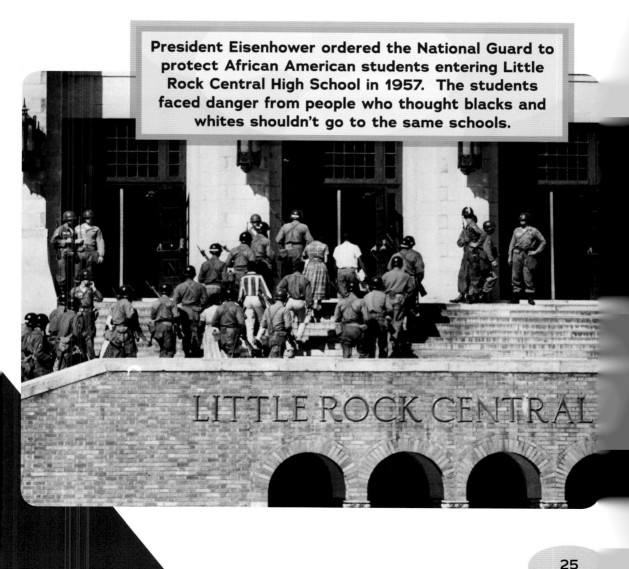

President Eisenhower ordered the National Guard to protect African American students entering Little Rock Central High School in 1957. The students faced danger from people who thought blacks and whites shouldn't go to the same schools.

Filling Jobs

The president's duties include choosing people for government jobs too. In many cases, the Senate must approve these choices. The president chooses Supreme Court judges, for example. But the Senate approves the choices.

The nine Supreme Court judges pose for a group picture in 2010. The Senate approved each of the judges.

Besides choosing judges, presidents have other legal powers. They can grant pardons. A person receiving a pardon is forgiven for committing a crime.

President George W. Bush pardons a turkey on Thanksgiving in 2007. Pardoning a turkey is a fun Thanksgiving Day presidential tradition.

Chapter 5

FOREIGN POLICY

The president's powers go beyond the United States. The president's foreign policy decisions affect the country's relationship with other nations.

President Woodrow Wilson (RIGHT) meets with foreign leaders in 1919. Sometimes presidents send other officials to represent the U.S. government in other countries. What are these officials called?

President George W. Bush shakes hands with Ronald Neumann, the U.S. ambassador to Afghanistan, in 2005.

The president has the power to choose ambassadors. A government sends these officials to represent it in another country. But the Senate has to approve the choices.

Working Together

At times, presidents have served as peacemakers.
They have helped other countries work out differences.

President Jimmy Carter (CENTER) brings together the leaders of Egypt (LEFT) and Israel (RIGHT) in 1979.

Presidents may encourage peace through foreign aid. Foreign aid is money or goods the United States gives other nations in hard times.

SOLDIERS IN THE U.S. ARMY
UNLOAD NEEDED SUPPLIES IN HAITI
AFTER AN EARTHQUAKE IN 2010.

The United States might give money or goods to help people after a flood or another disaster. If a country gets help from the United States, it may be more likely to listen to the president's ideas for peace.

A U.S. Navy soldier helps a boy carry relief items in Indonesia in 2005 after the country was hit by a tsunami (huge wave).

Chapter 6

COMMANDER IN CHIEF

As the leader of the military, the president chooses high-level military officers. But Congress has to approve the choices. The president can also choose to increase or decrease the military's size. Congress approves these decisions too.

The president chooses high-level military officers such as General Martin Dempsey. But the president doesn't choose them alone. Who must approve the decision?

Wars

The president is responsible for defending the country in times of war or peace. Only Congress can declare war. But presidents can send troops to fight overseas. They can do so even when no war has been declared.

President Franklin Roosevelt signs Congress's declaration of war against Japan in 1941.

President Harry S. Truman spoke on TV in 1950 about the U.S. military's efforts in Korea.

Military missions ordered by the president don't always go well. Sometimes innocent people are hurt. Or bad weather or rough land keeps the military from completing its mission. The president must weigh the risks of missions against the possible gains.

Not Easy

The president's job is never easy. Presidents realize the importance of their work. Many presidents' decisions have helped make our nation great.

ABRAHAM LINCOLN WAS PRESIDENT DURING THE CIVIL WAR (1861–1865).

When you grow up, maybe you'll want to be president. Will you have what it takes? Only time will tell.

Future president Barack Obama is pictured here in the 1960s in Hawaii riding a tricycle.

Glossary

ambassador: a person sent by a government to represent it in another country

bill: a written plan for a new law

cabinet: the group of presidential advisers who head departments within the executive branch

citizen: a person who lives in a city, a state, or a country

Congress: a group of elected officials who write, discuss, and make laws. The U.S. Congress is made up of the Senate and the House of Representatives.

elect: to pick by voting

executive branch: the branch of government that is led by the president. The executive branch enforces the laws of the United States.

executive order: a rule or regulation called for by the president

foreign aid: money or goods that the United States gives to other nations

foreign policy: a country's general plan or principle for relating to other nations

impeach: to officially charge the president or other high official with serious wrongdoing

judicial branch: the branch of government involving the court system

legislative branch: the branch of government that makes laws

override: to cancel or stop

pardon: to officially forgive a crime

term: a definite or limited period of time

treaty: an agreement with another nation

veto: to reject a bill and keep it from becoming a law

Learn More about Government

Books

Donovan, Sandy. *Did President Grant Really Get a Ticket for Speeding in a Horse-Drawn Carriage?: And Other Questions about U.S. Presidents.* Minneapolis: Lerner Publications Company, 2011. Check out this book to find the answers to some fun questions about our nation's presidents.

Jakubiak, David J. *What Does the President Do?* New York: PowerKids Press, 2010. Learn more about the executive branch and the president's duties.

Stier, Catherine. *If I Ran for President.* Morton Grove, IL: Albert Whitman, 2007. Six children explain the election process in this lively book.

Sutcliffe, Jane. *Barack Obama.* Minneapolis: Lerner Publications Company, 2010. Read the life story of Barack Obama, from his childhood in Hawaii and Indonesia to his election as president of the United States.

Websites

Ben's Guide to U.S. Government for Kids
http://bensguide.gpo.gov/3-5/index.html
This website includes lots of useful information about the U.S. government.

Enchanted Learning: The Presidents of the United States of America
http://www.enchantedlearning.com/history/us/pres/list.shtml
Visit this site to see a chronological list of U.S. presidents. You'll also find information about the White House, tips for writing a letter to the president, and crafts related to the presidents.

WayBack: Presidents
http://pbskids.org/wayback
This site features kids' thoughts on what it takes to be president. Fun secrets about U.S. presidents and information about what it's like to run for president are also included.

Index

Photo Acknowledgments

The images in this book are used with the permission of: © Time Life Pictures/National Archives/Getty Images, p. 4; Library of Congress pp. 5 (LC-DIG-ppbd-00358/Souza, Pete), 11 (LC-USZC4 488/Robert Pryor), 22 (LC-USZ62-95480); © Roberto Schmidt/AFP/Getty Images, p. 6; © Bettmann/CORBIS, p. 7; © Joshua Roberts/Bloomberg via Getty Images, p. 8; © Gene Forte/Consolidated News Pictures/Getty Images, p. 9; © Wally McNamee/CORBIS, pp. 10, 23, 24; © Chris Harris/WPA Pool/Getty Images, p. 12; © Three Lions/Stringer/Hulton Archives/Getty Images, p. 13; National Archives pp. 14 (ARC Identifier 1667751), 28 (ARC Identifier 530791); © Owen Franken/CORBIS, p. 15; © Universal Images Group/Universal History Archive/Hutlon Archive/Getty Images, p. 16; © Dirck Halstead/Time Life Pictures/Getty Images, p. 17; © Kristoffer Tripplaar/Alamy, p. 18; © CORBIS, p. 19; © Scott J. Ferrell/CQ-Roll Call Group/Congressional Quarterly/Getty Images, p. 20; © Universal History Archive/Hulton Archive/Getty Images, p. 21; © Bettmann/CORBIS, p. 25; © Jim Lo Scalzo/epa/CORBIS, p. 26; © Jason Reed/Reuters/CORBIS, p. 27; © Paul Morse/White House via Getty Images, p. 29; © David Rubinger/Time Life Pictures/Getty Images, p. 30; © Mike Greenslade/Alamy, p. 31; © Udo Weitz/Bloomberg via Getty Images, p. 32; AP Photo/Susan Walsh, p. 33; © World History Archive/Alamy, p. 34; AP Photo/Henry Griffin, p. 35; © Courtesy of the National Archives/Newsmakers/Getty Images, p. 36; © Obama for America/Handout/Reuters/CORBIS, p. 37.
Front Cover: AP Photo/Gerald Herbert.

Main body text set in Adrianna Regular 14/20
Typeface provided by Chank